FAUNA

ACKNOWLEDGMENTS

Grateful acknowledgement is made to the following publications in which some of the poems in this collection first appeared, sometimes in different versions: *Bearing Witness: The Best of the Observer Arts Literary Magazine:* "The Scene of Mutiny"; "Island Women"; "My Father's Mother"; "Fauna"; *Calabash: A Journal of Caribbean Arts and Letters:* "Calabash"; "Calling Me Back Home"; "Girl" (honorable mention in the Literary Arts Competition); "Before Electricity"; "Pa" (winner of the Literary Arts Competition); "Full Bloom"; *The Caribbean Writer:* "Flowers of The Caribbean" (honorable mention in the Literary Arts Competition)*; Crab Orchard Review:* "My Great Grandmother" (winner of the Literary Arts Competition); "Xaymaca"; *Die Aussensites Des Elementes:* "My Great Grandmother Speaks To Me"; "The Apple Tree"; "Au Pair"; *The Glistening Stars:* "Recurring Dream"*; The Jamaica Observer Arts Magazine:* "My Father: A Snapshot"; "The Scene of Mutiny"; "Fauna"; "Island Women"; "My Father's Mother"; *MaComère:* "Lilith Speaks"; "Eve & Lilith"; "Snakes"; "The Smell of Mango"; *Renaissance Noire:* "Leaving the Noise of the World Behind"; "Jamaican Birds"; *Wasafiri:* "The Picture." Some of the information in the poem "Calabash" was obtained from the book, *Flowers of the Caribbean*, by G.W. Lennox & S.A. Seddon; and in the poem "Fauna" from *Birds of Jamaica* by Audrey Downer & Robert Sutton.

I thank Sharon Olds for working and then working again with me on many of these poems; Donna Masini for teaching me "new ways of listening" to a poem; Lorna Goodison for the example of herself and for being a really good teacher and a kind person over the years; Sandra Pouchet Paquet and the folks at the Caribbean Writers Summer Institute at the University of Miami for five truly amazing weeks; Wayne Brown for publishing my work and telling me, "I think you're a really good writer." Shara McCallum too for the example of herself and for listening and loving and being *very* supportive; Deborah Digges and the late William Matthews. I thank Catharine Stimpson and Karen Singleton for more things than I would be able to put into words; Stacy Ann Blair, Susan (I'm in such a state!) Brennan, Peggy Garrison, Adam McConnel, Dolace Nicole McLean & Yvonne Murphy for listening and listening and then listening some more; Jeremy Poynting for taking the chance; My father, Michael Johnson, who I have come to be able to talk with about many things, including poetry. My mother and my grandmother. The spirit and soul of my great grandparents, Celeste and Ferdinand Walker, pervade these poems.

FAUNA

poems

JACQUELINE BISHOP

PEEPAL TREE

First published in Great Britain in 2006
Peepal Tree Press Ltd
17 King's Avenue
Leeds LS6 1QS
UK

ISBN 1 84523 032 9

Peepal Tree gratefully acknowledges Arts Council support

For
My great grandparents
Ferdinand & Celeste Walker
In memoriam

CONTENTS

III.

IV.

Turning and turning in the widening gyre
W.B. YEATS

LOT'S WIFE

Some say it was for vanity,
others that it was for greed—
this woman who ended up
a great corroding consuming
body of salt, this woman, who,
like me, is always looking back.

I

AN END, OR MAYBE A BEGINNING

All good things, my grandmother tells me,
must come to an end – a closing

of the circle of myth and memory, or perhaps,
just a beginning. And who is to say

I am remembering it right . . . after . . . after . . .
God knows how many years!

There was no island-paradise; or perhaps there was:
I cannot remember any more. I cannot remember.

This must have been how Eve felt
that first time out of the garden;

one story running into another.

Father, forgive me for the stories I tell –
the stories I had to tell.

This, after all, was the meaning of your life:
your admonition to me:

Tell it and tell it again, your story,
to whomever, my daughter, will stop and listen.

Nights my great grandfather sat on the darkened verandah of memory
looking out into the ink-blue sky. I would be curled at his feet,
a great dark cat. He would tell me then how he came to be in this place,
how he had met my great grandmother, the life they built together:
"I was a young man then, and there was nothing doing in Hanover.
Already I had fathered two children and I spent my days carousing
the streets and drinking. Someone told me there was work in Portland,
and I packed my bags and came. I was a strapping young lad then,

adventurous, with a simple plan of making enough money
and returning home. I did not know I would never see that life
again, would never see my parents again, and only one sister
would follow me here. I have often wondered about those first two
children – they must be grown people by now, children,
grandchildren, of their own. When I met your great grandmother
she was nothing much to look at, all arms and legs.
From the start she was a difficult woman, set in her ways,
unwilling to bend; a true Jamaican woman. We were married

one year later: she was sixteen, I was twenty-one.
I then worked these sugar cane fields. Over the years
life has been fairly good to us: we own the house we live in,
eight of our twelve children still alive. Can you believe
after sixty-one years that woman still has a temper?"
He would stop talking then, lean into his chair, I would draw
even closer to him. The stink-sweet smell of a ripe jackfruit
hung heavy in the air around us. His hair silver-white,
mottled skin covered with brown spots. The tiny
kerosene lamp on the verandah was the only light for miles.

THE PICTURE

Lean bamboos along a country road.
Clustered dark trunks,
pale light of the sun.
The picture opens to a figure on the left,
strong in the moment of her life,
my great grandmother,
arms akimbo at her side.
White blouse, floral printed skirt,
yards of cloth wrapped tight around her head –
two green leaves within the folds of her head-wrap:
protection against things evil.
Face darkened, features indistinct,
death reconfigures all her parts,
but stills an essence as the river,
silvery-blue through the gossiping bamboos.
And there! Up the street walking down,
three young girls,
jugs of water on their heads,
the earth rising in an upsweep of young shoots
making way for these laughing girls.
All my mysteries reside in this place,
small dot of an island,
the restlessness and the need to always return
to my great grandmother's river.
Last night I dreamt that a woman,
who was not my great grandmother,
folded a cup of thick green leaves
filled with river water for me to drink.
She brought this sacrament to my lips with dark hands,
able hands, my great grandmother's hands.

There she stands – there we stand –
arms akimbo – three jugs of water,

outlined in yellow.

MY GREAT GRANDMOTHER SPEAKS TO ME

Twelve times my waters broke
Over these blue Jamaican mountains –

only eight of my children surviving;
my other four: the dust of these mountains.

I've watched you over the years,
saw a restless dark behind your eyes.

I've watched you and knew: Some day,
she will unfold, acres and acres of blood-red bracts.

Now I'll tell you something
I've never told anyone before:

On the day you were born I planted
at the base of these mountains

your navel-string which blossomed
a patch of first flowers.

Those flowers were for you, in honour,
my very own – red ginger.

GIRL

"Listen,
cocoa pods grow green,
ripen yellow,
		mature purple,
burst them open with a stone –
look, like this –
eat the soft white insides;

"Or grind them in a mortar
until the cocoa is your color,
roll into balls,
put to sun,
drink cocoa-tea hot in the mornings.

"Now be careful star-apples –
them will bind you up.
The big tree at the edge of our land
		bear only purple fruit –
some trees only green fruit.
Break the star-apple open,
		eat the white part,
		stay far from the pink part –
bind you bad girl.

"At night you walking,
let somebody call you twice before you answer –
never answer a first call.
Turn 'round twice you pass silk-cotton tree.
Rolling Calf start to run you down,
make sure you reach junction before it –
lie down like a star.

"Spirits can take the shape of animals,
if you ever catch a fish that is too big,
have eyes that look strange,
put it back where you get it from.
Don't carry home stray animals,
one start to follow you home –
spin two times to confuse it.

"Sunday you going to church, cover your head.
And I hope your mother don't have you going
those none-soul churches in Kingston.
Learn first to dance a yard
before you dance abroad.
Keep your head up high,
you will go far,
you is your great grandma's child."

PRELUDE

This was how we came to know him:
the person whose back was forever turned to us;

My father — *Our Father* —

the master painter
in-front of a stark white canvas.

He never seemed to get it right,
could never paint us back — once and for all —
— the genesis —
his beautiful garden.

Everyday he kept at it, his back hunched
as he leaned into the canvas, fingers gnarled,
placing brushstroke after careful brushstroke.

He kept at it even as the walls of our house buckled
under its own weight.

I came to know him as the man my mother hushed us around;
forbade us to talk to as he worked, as he searched,
for something he would never find.

I am his daughter:
I am she who is always seeking.

MY FATHER: A SNAPSHOT

I have very few pictures
of him, and whatever

pictures I do have,
are never in focus.

They are as blurry
as my eyes would

eventually become.
This condition

I inherited from him.

My father is the man
who is always

at the edge
of the photograph;

The man who is
barely smiling;

The man who is never
looking straight at the camera.

MY FATHER'S MOTHER

Speaks to me in a language
I do not understand –

comes to me in my dream,
wearing a dress the colour of the
Caribbean sky.

She is a caramel-colored
woman – heavy set,

wavy black hair
pulled tight in a bun.

She frowns, then smiles,
then reaches for me.

RECURRING DREAM

Neon-blue light surrounds me.
I shudder. I gleam. Terrible gulled fish.

Someone is out to get me!

I wade through mud, morass, cracked shells.

Large black cats, backs arched, stretched,
are out prowling
their guttural territorial growls.

LITTER

We had been warned not to touch them or their mother would
    abandon them –
the slick wet coats of young kittens just birthed. For weeks we watched

as our cat's belly swelled and sagged, watched as she, at first, moved less
    swiftly, then not at all.
It was difficult for her to sit still, to sleep; all positions were uncomfortable.

When I, her favourite, came close with a bowl of milk she hissed
and clawed. I imagined the milk going down into her swollen body,
    stimulating

her own production; when I saw her heavy rose-pink nipples I knew,
relief would come with each kitten suckling. Some days she allowed
    me to stroke her,

to reach over and pull her onto my lap. Then one morning,
    at dawn,
I followed a trail of blood and frail new cries out of the house and into
    the back yard where I found

her, licking each of five kittens. I couldn't resist the urge
to reach out and touch them, to pull them from their mother's tit
    and take them,

one by one, into my arms, as if I could be their deep seeking source,
    as if
my young dark body could give them milk. I was unprepared
    for how she would,

from that moment henceforth, have nothing to do with
    the kittens, and
what followed afterwards: my own desperate attempts to save them,
    to fill them,

with something other than milk. For years I blamed myself for the
     weakening
kittens, each one I placed into a shallow grave. I did not realize then
     what I had been reaching for –

my own mother long lost to me, the woman who,
     for years, I had not seen
not felt, not touched; I was reaching for my brothers
     as we would

climb over each other, legs and arms all a-tangle; each, now,
     like stars,
spilling from the dark sky.

THE SMELL OF MANGO

I am seven years old.
My grandfather and I
are in my mother's bedroom.
There is a large oakwood bed
in the centre of the room
made up with pink and white ruffles.
At the window,
a shy blue curtain is blowing;
through wide glass window panes
yellow sun floods the room.
Let me tell you about the smell of mango,
I can even tell you about the silence
within the room
as my grandfather
raises himself up,
pulls the zipper of his pants.
I am so afraid.
Let me tell you about
the darknesses which descend over me.

SNAKES

All those years when my mother knew exactly
what my grandfather was doing, she knew,
and she let it continue. Her excuse: *It happened to me too.*
After my grandmother had left him, had packed her things
and moved out, he complained of being lonely,
said he wanted a girl to help about the house.
I begged her not to send me, peed on myself, hollered,
rolled in the dirt, told her how he spooned-up
against me at night, his hot breath quickening
around my neck. How frightened
I was of his darkened contorted face. Then the touch
of those rough, callused hands, reaching for
my breasts – the shame of them –
the revulsion of them – I wished they would stay buried
within my body. Then the sudden sharp pain
of those large knobbed fingers between my legs. It was then
that I learnt to hate myself, to feel different,
to know that something was wrong
with me. She taught me to take it, to forgive my grandfather
and take it. She taught me that this was what it meant
to be a woman. I did not know how to name
what my mother and my grandfather had done to me,
until that day at the zoo when I saw them, a family,
curled around each other, saw the venomous tongues that darted
and flickered, the evil intent in their glowing red eyes.

II

FLAME TREE

I am tired of this, arms outstretched
providing shade
from the unrelenting sun. I am tired
of my clusters of orange/red blossoms,
tired of being beautiful for you. Try to imagine
being on your feet all your life, meddlesome
creatures nesting in your hair.
Outdoors in a hurricane,
clinging to your roots for dear life,
I long for those days, old woman that I am,
when my feather-like leaves have withered and fallen away,
leaving only the rattling seed pods called woman's-tongue,
shaking and shaking in the wind.

ALLAMANDA

Of course it was necessary, you fool,
standing there in judgment of me,
calling me a lunatic
as you lay the child's corpse at my feet.
Everything alive develops a defense,
some way of protecting itself.
Mine is poison; all parts of me are toxic.
I had no way of discerning
it was a child's hand,
I only knew the touch was human
and deadly, reaching out to pluck
my yellow blossoms.

LOVE BUSH

Those nights I would creep over the walls,
shameless in my desire for you,
carrying a profusion
of blush-pink blossoms,
they thought I had lost my mind,
I, the teacher, the old maid,
had forsaken my own pupils
for the touch of you.
My petals are not fully developed;
I am, as you know, a late bloomer.
But that time at the fence
you were so surprised
how I had grown, and grown,
dense masses of dull-green heart-shaped leaves
slowly overtaking your body.

IXORA

Why must you pout like that?
Why must you put on that showy red dress,
go down to the Bay where the men will gape at you?

Why can't you be the good Catholic girl,
the flower in white,
all that your mother wanted you to be?

Or, if you insist on that bright red colour,
why can't you be more like red ginger –
hide your true flowers within?

Do you know what they say about you
Behind your back? Do you know the names
They call you?

Flame-of-the-Wood, Jungle Flame, Jungle Geranium.

I have been sent by the good women
of the church to ask of you:
Be done with the drinking, the swearing,
the staggering home at night.

Put away those shimmering emerald earrings
you call leaves.
Tame that brick-red hair.

Come back
from living by yourself
at the edge of the woods.

Your kind – our kind, Ixora,
prefer being bunched together, forming
a large spherical head, all of us

whispering.

PERIWINKLE

Aren't you tired of it?
Aren't you tired of flowering
all the time –

five virgin-white petals
meeting in your darker centre,
and always the circular pattern?

Aren't you tired of listening to the nuns?
Placing us in groups:
so many good women!

Our Lady of Lasalette;
Our Lady of Fatima;
Our Lady of Lourdes.

I remember you, Periwinkle,
from the front of the class
your slender raised hand –

and always the same joke: Ixora,
did *you* do your homework last night?
But tell me, really,

don't you ever get tired of it?
The stupid grin, the girl
from Madagascar always laughing?

ANTHURIUM

Large red heart-shaped waxy bract,
who would've thought that you –
the pick of all the boys –

Flamingo Flower, Heart Flower,

you, with your pale-pink
spadix, so resembling

an erect penis, you
who got all the attention:

Put Anthurium, always, in the centre of the table!

Who would've though that you
would fade so fast.

Now I'm not the only one who knows
your cruel laugh, your taunts,

how quickly you change face,
put on the demure peasant girl from South America,

the one with the halting English,
the one you carried, carefully concealed, to Jamaica.

You have married badly, your six children,
are against you. No more:

What a beautiful, exotic-looking flower!

OLEANDER

You tell me:
What should I have done?

You tell me:
What would you have done?

Those fingers of his –
tall and pointed as my green leaves –
he would not stop touching me.

As soon as night came with its great big feet
and the Missis turned in off the verandah –

(Tell me, don't you think she knew what was going on,
his eyes following me wherever I went?

Him always sojourning out after dark
to check on the slaves) –

he would be at the door,
and my mother, she forced me out to him.

So you can stand there, angry knot of a crowd,
judge me all you want.

Would it make a difference if I told you
it started at a very young age?

I carried the poison deep within the folds of the pink dress
he gave me last Christmas. The one
he loved to see me in.

The one, he said, he had taken all the way from a place
called the Mediterranean – *just for me.*

He kept saying how much I had grown.
That perhaps it was time to give me a pruning.

He wanted to know if he was the only one –
how should I put this – getting his fill of me.

The hesitation in my eyes:
It made him angry. Very angry.

(Missis, I am not lying, your husband was saying and doing
these things to me!)

You say I am unrepentant.
That I will hang for what I have done.

Tell me:
What is there to fear

when you no longer fear
death?

CANNA LILY

For example, my daughter, the one
from the private girl's school in Kingston;

my daughter, who I see from time to time
on the grainy black-and-white television set –

                    always in a fabulous red dress;

the senator's wife,
house on the hill, two daughters

who I never see;
my daughter who cannot understand

my love of moist places – out in the wild –
and why I could never

spend my life in any of the now-popular public parks,
or, like her, in someone's private garden.

PETREA

Mexican
woman
with bushy blue hair,

oftentimes I watch you
by the river
— washing.

You are always
slightly apart
from the others.

When the spirit takes you,
you hum,
sometimes sing

a long forgotten song.
They do not like it,
how you do not

concern yourself
with being showy.
Your wise dull

dark-green eyes —
how you cherish
solitude!

Their constant,
insistent,
murmuring.

FULL BLOOM
For L.G.

For every breath you take

may a canna lily
bloom

For every time your hands
guide the birth of a poem

hibiscus flower

For every time your green-giving voice
comforts another

heliconia

For every time you recite
one of your prayer/poems

red ginger

CALABASH

This tree
grows to a height
of about thirty feet. The
branches are long and form a
spreading habit. The characteristic
arrangement of the leaves is in clustered
or condensed spirals on reduced shoots
borne on long thin branches. Each leaf is
between two and five inches long, their texture
is leathery, the colour bright green on the upper
surface and paler below. Flowers are bell-shaped,
each about two inches with a pale or dark yellow
colour. The fruits are globular in shape and large
specimens may grow to more than twelve inches
in diameter. The central pulp and seeds are
often removed, leaving a hard woody shell;
such structures are watertight and are
frequently used for holding liquid (they
are called gourds) and they are also
used as ornaments. The calabash
is a native of the
Caribbean

III

THE RAFT OF THE MEDUSA

For Peter Homitzky

My teacher says:
Artists, as we know, are people

profoundly disturbed
by the world —

so disturbed,
they seek to remake it.

I think about this constantly,
my paintbrush poised:

What to put in?
What to leave out?

THE SCENE OF MUTINY

The figure of the young girl is lovely,
And it is almost an exception to the great master's work.[1]

The studies that have survived
show a dying or exhausted mother, a meditative father

and a nude child, his dark hair
blowing in the wind.

The boat is crowded. Everyone is in rags.
There is not much space.

Only a few can survive.
Study after study Géricault makes decisions,

leaving in what is essential, taking out what
is not, much the same way that I am doing now.

In the final painting, the woman is gone, replaced
by a heroic couplet: a father and a son.

1. Said of Géricault's painting "a Pareleytic Woman" by his first
biographer, Charles Clément.

AU PAIR
For Marina

We startled pigeons into flight at *Gare*
St. Lazare. We held hands through
the streets of the *Quatrième Arrondissement*,
Russian girl, eyes the colour
of my Jamaican waters;
knocking my *chambre-de-bonne*,
late one night, shaded
white candle in your slender left hand.

I did not know that I would hold you,
pale and shivering in my arms, stroke you
after the baby Philipe never wanted.
You were so cold;
he never came once to the hospital.

Sometimes, stormy silences,
and once we passed each other
"like strangers" on *Rue St. Vincent*.
But my last day in Paris,
curled into each other's summer arms,
sheer curtain blowing against
hard wood-brown table;
yellow daffodils on that table. . .

THE APPLE TREE

For Linda McCarriston

She would leave by the back door,
using light from the moon,
go by the structure where the family showered
in the evenings:
            slender green bamboo slit down the middle,
and going brown;
banana plants hung with the burden of rotting fruit;
sugarcane swaying and rustling in the cool night's air.

She was on her way to the apple tree,
            seeing it from whatever distance –
                        how beautiful it was.

They had grown up together, the girl
            and the apple tree,
bark widening
to her touch, boughs
enough to hide a slim young body.

The apple tree lived through droughts,
            the months no rain fell;
        she brought water from the river;
fed its flesh-starved roots.

The tree bloomed suddenly,
attracting a colony of feathered-white birds,
        beaks into ivory blossoms;
swarms of honey-colored bees.

And when he found where she was hiding,
            her grandfather came to the tree with a cutlass,
                there he stood making deals with a nine year old –
                        bud barely coming into flower.

And to save the life of the apple tree the girl surrendered her body.

The fruit the tree eventually bore;
the crowds that came to eat of it;
the many who found them and took them are fallen away.

CARNAGE

For Wangari Maathai

Up and down the streets they lie
   the first week in January –
      past usefulness; past the meaning of usefulness.

Chopped at the stems,
   flesh cut clear through with axe;
      seeing it is like pulling bark from myself.

I am there with the pine in the forest,
   roots pushing deeper and deeper into soil.
      Axe glistening and raised silver.

As it strikes, sap oozes out.
   The axe is raised and strikes again
      and again, digging further, digging faster.

And all the talk going on around me:
   of the ozone layer diminishing and the slow
      deadly warming of the earth.

Deserts keep spreading –
   ink let loose on paper.
      The rain forests are shrinking;

whole species of animals dying.
   Still we buy these trees every Christmas,
      take them home to our families

who come close, touch, the lush dark needles;
   smell for the clean clear scent of the country
      high in the cold mountains.

We do not think of the ozone layer and its deadly warming,
    nor the woman I read about in Kenya,
        back bent, planting trees into a greenbelt.

With one final blow the tree is felled.
    How we eat ourselves alive – roots, limbs, leaves;
        our blood, and the body which is bark.

DON'T YOU KNOW THIS WOMAN?

My name is Fibbah, Carribah, Abbenah,
Hannah, Lubbah, Quasheba –
        none of these my rightful names.
Superannuated slave,
grown past youthfulness,
            past the days I was prized
for the fruits of my labour; the fruits of my body.

Yes, you have heard this lament before;
still I keep asking:
Don't you know this woman?

Starting life in the pickaniny gang,
a child, under the supervision of Old Dinah,
I picked vines, carried water, on this estate,
graduated to weeding, grass picking.
Would that I could still the unfolding
        of my fifteen-year-old body from
the sharp scrutiny of your terrible eyes.

What was I worth then? My value
calculated in rations:
1 pt. ginger tea each morning,
2 lbs. roots;
5 lbs. potatoes,
2 lbs. saltfish.

As member of the first gang I cut,
bundled canes, hoed soil, dug drains,
pulled weeds from among canes,
in this increasingly infertile soil.
Thirty-five years in the first gang, and now,

approaching fifty, titties sagging from twelve children,
you tell me my manumission has been granted:
I must now fend-for-myself.
Massa, Backra, won't you look good at me,
        answer my question:
Don't you know this woman?

YOSHITOSHI'S WOMEN[2]

are sensitively
conceived,

are lavishly
executed.

Look at the details
on their flour-pale faces.

The time he must
have taken!

His prints are women
caught in the dailiness

of their daily lives:
combing

each other's long, dark
hair, serving tea

from a bright red kettle.
One or two of them

are crying.

2. Taiso Yoshitosh (1839-1892) Japanese woodcut printer.

JOAN OF ARC

No one took the time to record
the details about her –

the colour of her hair, her eyes.

Did she rest the weight
    of her body,
more on one side

than the other?
Did she have a slight limp? Or, like me,
A lazy left eye?

Would she sit some mornings, alone,
on her horse and watch
the sun slowly rising?

One question leads to another.

Flowers – did she love them –
the fat heads of dahlias
quietly nodding?

EVE & LILITH

for Yvonne.

No, I do not blame you for it,
and what you say is true: you did not create this world.

You were only born of it, as Eve was born of it,
as was Lilith before her, the demon figure.

You did not will for yourself a pale skin,
nor I my dark skin; and neither

of us is responsible for what others
choose to make of this. Our responsibilities are to ourselves,

to the daily lives we lead;
there is still so much work to be done.

I know that sometimes you wish you had been the dark one,
the one who, you say, got away.

I ask you again: Could you live forever in this body?
proferring the same pendulous breasts

over and over again to the world, only now
they are greatly shrunken and withered and have nothing more to give.

You are right about this:
We are both looking for mothering. I confess,

I have always wanted to return to the folds of the earth.

But today on the telephone, I heard your despair:
That you wish to be seen in your own right, that you are tired

of being an object, a trophy, a multi-coloured parrot
in someone's gilded cage.

Wasn't this always the argument between the women of my family
And the women of yours?

Never mind, you will fly.
You will fly! Your wings

have not, despite what they tell you, been clipped.
There is still much of your Irish grandmother in you,

the one hidden away in the attic,
visible only from the high window,

who motioned me over with gnarled fingers.
When I refused to go to her, she started pacing again.

What was I to have done?
I had been told we were so different.

Now I think of Eve's decision to listen to the snake,
to eat of the tree of knowledge –

her bravery in approaching the unknown.

LILITH SPEAKS

I am she who you do not know.
I am she of the dark face,

the first wife, the example,
the one whispered about in tattered

and un-translated texts,
so carefully hidden in the stacks

that even the head librarian, the one
who knows everything, she who first arrived

with peachy good looks,
who is now a withered prune,
cannot locate.

Adam and I, we were both so young then –
trembling in the garden.

Why did he listen to The Father?
Insisting that I lay beneath him!

I took it and took it, until finally, after years,
I got up out of myself,
flew away to the Red Sea.

Reader,
the book you hold in your hand is old,

the pages are crumbling.
The woman they say is me, the succubus,

the woman of filth,
is a face distorted and turned onto itself.

Reader,
won't you take this frail hand,

these tired bones,
lead it out of this maze, these lonely stacks.

ISLAND JUICE BLEND

Make of me a label,
one of your fruit-juice concoctions
on which you hang the word *exotic*.
At my breasts and sex: yellow bananas.
Let me carry a calabash
of papayas, naseberries and star-apples,
my smile outlined in the most extravagant red.
Eyes darkly kholed;
hibiscus flower behind my left ear.
Here I stand –
all hips and thighs.
Read the fine print on the label: Authentic –
we make our juices with only the best tropical fruits –
tart, tangy, sun-ripened pineapples,
substantial amounts of passion fruit added to the blend.
No artificial flavours;
no preservatives added.
Serve chilled over crushed ice, preferably with
a dash of one-hundred-proof Jamaican rum.

ISLAND WOMEN

I know that even though I know more than my grandparents,
I will never be as wise — Toni Morrison.

I wonder if they
somehow knew —

all those women —

some of whom,
in all probability, could not

read what I am
writing right now.

I wonder if they all
secretly knew

in the storage closets
of their chests

that one day
they would have

a daughter, a
granddaughter, a
great granddaughter, and
more,

who would come asking
questions?

IV

CALLING ME BACK HOME
for the muse

(i)
When she thought no one was looking
she removed the dress they had given her,
crawled naked into the river.
Men later insisted
they saw something silver in the sunlight
    – looked like fish scales –
one even said it had grown a tail.

(ii)
(My Great Grandmother had warned me
not to walk alone in the bushes,
not to talk to strangers
– especially not women in the bushes –
and never to look into water.)

(iii)
She stepped from behind
a tree,
small dark woman,
chain of teeth around her neck,
locked hair, webbed hands and feet.
She called me to the river's edge,
"Come dance with your water self," she said,
standing in white mist near blue falls.

(iv)
(It was said I was lost for two weeks in the bushes.)

(v)
When I went over
she took me by the hand,
we watched our shadowed selves
on the water's surface,
        then I heard it:
voice like a woman sighing,
        or singing.
We looked into the water,
then jumped in.

(vi)
I was afraid,
the dark and the deep
        – a frightening feel
of falling –
she held me close,
my head against her bosom,
until we got to the bottom,
where she fed me roots and herbs
that made me sleep.

(vii)
The men from my district came –
        trucks, vans, chain-saws –
uprooted trees,
tried filling the river with stones
to ensure another girl-child
would not be lost to them.
Every year the forest claimed a woman.

(viii)
They found us
entwined, covered in green leaves
at the bottom of the river
and pulled us apart.

I held onto a memory:
circle of women,
fire, black cat with green eyes,
silver moon,
voices raised in singing.

(viiii)
We were taken back to the district,
her hair was cut.
Still she hungered
for nakedness, roots, herbs, locked hair
and the first chance she got
made her way back to the river.

(x)
As for me
I do not walk by bushes
without hearing a woman's voice singing,
pass a body of water and not see
a familiar shape
small and dark
calling me back home.

THE MOUNTAIN IN THE DISTANCE
For My Mother

In
the distance
there is a mountain
I am reaching for; contained
within this mountain is the jewel;
the jeweled part of myself that is always
seeking, seeking for the mother and her
mountain; the mountain my mother, the mother-
mountain which searches for the mother's land, the
mother-land. Africa is the mountain in the distance.
Mother-Africa is the mountain in the distance *is*
my mother and her tongue. The mountain in the distance
holds my mother's tongue, holds my mother-tongue.
My mother-tongue and the island to which the child was
taken from the mother; the child was exiled to the island
Jamaica and forged a new language with another; now
the child is a woman and soon to be a mother; she will give to
her child the language of the Ancestor; kept alive in the hybrid
fusion, the daughter who will soon become a mother to the island
of Jamaica. Mother-mountain in the distance   mountain in the distance
which is the landofmymother whichisAfrica Africa landofmymothertongue.

XAYMACA

One of the islands of the archipelago,
which arcs the Caribbean,
my mother is the island between Cuba
and Santo Domingo – *Xaymaca* –

land of wood and water,
named by those who first peopled her – *Tainos* –
peaceful people, it is for them, now extinct
that mother's tears

spill down the backbone blue mountains,
collecting the blue of these mountains,
bringing them down to her amniotic harbour waters –
its distinct shade of aquamarine.

Mother's all-seeing eye is the moon,
pale and full, over Kingston,
taking in, in cool detachment,
all laid bare before her.

When she is satisfied with what she sees
mother pulls a cloak over her darkened body
and sleeps. Mother's teeth
have sharpened into reefs

against those who would enter
and deflower her gardens.
As did marauders, who
buccaneered her fertile brown body,

razed the landscape.
Mother tallied the injustices,
cracked into an earthquake –
the year was 1692.

She left only one survivor to tell the tale.
Still, so much of what *Xaymaca* knows
is submerged: folded into
her jeweled sex; underwater.

MY GREAT GRANDMOTHER

Finally I just gave up and became
my great grandmother,
packed my college degrees,
fellowships and travels abroad
into a suitcase,
left New York for Jamaica
to become
a seller of cow's milk,
woman smelling always of nutmeg and pimento
who lived all her life in the same district,
everyone kin to you.
My hands would pull the thick
skin easily from green bananas
and I would love one man
for all but the first sixteen
years of my life.
I would become the woman
who could withstand
whatever life brought –
no tears shed in public –
and in the evenings
watering my garden
my twelve children about me,
pot of something cooking.

Small house backed by blue dark hills
started out one-room board shack.
Mortar around it   cement added –
bedroom   verandah   living room;
was still unfinished when my Great Grandfather died,
never got as big as he wanted.
Now grass fills the house up.

To the right of the house, earth dropped;
To the left, earth rose;
stones were packed against the down side,
        that we would not fall over,
lose ourselves to the leaves –
                so many fruit trees.

        Do you remember:
            we sat quietly, waiting
for an avocado to fall,
roll on down the down.
How we scrambled –
            all ten-twelve of us –
            to get the avocado first!
Do you remember that, Pa?

Near the out-house,
            big nutmeg tree –
dark brown nuts,
            cream/yellow skin
we tried forcing open.

            – *No need to do that:*
            the nutmeg will come open in its own good time!

How we'd come rolling from the up,
that thick green grass,
thickest in the world, Pa,
        greenest too,
        Ma chasing us with a stick,
 *Grass stains are the hardest in the world
            to get out!*

Now I stand in the old
abandoned house, shout your name
to the dark blue mountains.
Not even an echo returns.

Don't you remember,
                remember,
                        remember me, Pa?

JAMAICAN BIRDS

You will find them everywhere,
numbered bands on their legs
tracing the route of their migratory flight.
I know a family of Jamaican birds,
the mother bird and four of her five baby birds
are in the United States;
the father has remained in Jamaica.
There is a brother bird in Toronto
along with an aunt bird, and two niece birds.
One of the birds in the family is skittish,
she is forever flying off somewhere,
for a while she lived in Paris
and one night, watching television,
saw birds from her island being interviewed
from their nests in Holland!
Large colonies of Jamaican birds
are dispersed all over the Caribbean,
many went to build the Panama Canal,
and some have even retraced the flight across the Atlantic.
In North America three or four species
have been identified by the peculiar way they sing.

FAUNA

There are 200 species and 50+ vagrants
on the island of Jamaica.
25 of the birds on the island
are endemic species;
21 endemic subspecies;
4 introduced species.
High levels of endemism on
Caribbean islands is the result
of geographic isolation.
Some of the birds that arrived
on the island, by chance, evolved into new species.
There are 74 winter visitors
from North America, 18 of which
increase local breeding.
In addition to the 50 vagrants,
25 species are transients
or winter visitors, making this a population
of migrants, transients and vagrants.

MYTH

For Y.C.

Perhaps in a hundred years they will write about this:
the day we went to the Metropolitan Museum's
show on Vincent van Gogh.
One of us was late; the biographer will slyly hint it was me,
since I am the one who is always late.
They will not know you were dressed all in black,
that I wore bright orange nail polish, that before
we went in we sat under a tree,
outside the Museum, drinking diet cokes;
chasing each other's blues.
We were both married then, and one of us
would make a quick run, at the end of the day,
to collect her husband's clothing. The young cashier
who took our monies will remember how we stood out
among the thousands thronging the Museum.
She will say, when they track her down sixty
years later, old and bent, dying of emphysema,
that there was something special
about us, something edged in the yellow
of sunflowers. Her breasts
will no longer be firm and young,
one of Gaugin's mythical Tahitian nymphs,
but instead wrung dry from grief and children.
Our biographer will talk about how anxious I was to get in
to see the van Gogh's, that you, at least, were more patient,
took your time to absorb and savour what was about you,
the lingering path informing our trail.
We went after to Central Park, talked poetry, women's
creativity, the blues and greens of our world,
both of us fighting obscurity, struggling to birth visions.
van Gogh and Gaugin must have struggled
in the yellow house at *Auvers,*
how Vincent always wanted community —

this before he cut his ear off in desperation when Gaugin moved on;
before the black crows started circling in and over Vincent,
mixing the memories; before the enduring
myth overtook both artists and they started to spin
slowly away from each other and out into the world.

LEAVING THE NOISE OF THE WORLD BEHIND

At first you cannot get used to it –
New York City and its constant turning,
cars up and down the roadways
which split the city into its languages.
You cannot get used
to the hum of the refrigerator,
blue glare and talking heads from the television,
sounds of sirens, horns, radios;
feet shuffling, restless
under the windowsill.
You complain to the other bedraggled plant in the room,
who, like yourself, is thirsting for the soil of another country,
that New York City is not a place
where one should remain.
Still you find yourself one day,
head bent low and muttering,
in conversation with the revising poem –
the quiet of such moments;
the noise of the world fallen away.

Peepal Tree Press publishes a wide selection of outstanding fiction, poetry, drama, history and literary criticism with a focus on the Caribbean and its diaspora.

Ask for our free catalogues

Visit the Peepal Tree website and buy online at:

www.peepaltreepress.com

17 King's Avenue, Leeds LS6 1QS, United Kingdom
contact@peepaltreepress.com
tel: 44 (0)113 245 1703

Recent & forthcoming Poetry

Opal Palmer Adisa, *Caribbean Passion*, 1-900715-92-9, £7.99
Feisty, sensuous — and always thought provoking. Whether she is writing about history, family, Black lives, about love and sexual passion, there is an acute eye for the contraries of experience.

Opal Palmer Adisa, *I Name me Name: Lola*, 1-84523-044-2, £8.99
March 2007 Autobiography, dramatic monologues, lyrical observations, encomiums, prose poems and prophetic rants enact the construction of an identity that encompasses inner 'i-ness', gender, race, geography, the spiritual, the social and the political.

Merle Collins, *Lady in a Boat*, 1-900715-85-6, £7.99
Twenty years after the death of the Grenadian revolution, Merle Collins writes of a Caribbean adrift, amnesiac and in danger of nihilistic despair. But she also achieves a life-enhancing and consoling perspective on those griefs.

David Dabydeen, *Slave Song*, 1-84523-004-3, £7.99
Songs of frustration and defiance from African slaves and displaced Indian laborers are expressed in a harsh and lyrical Guyanese Creole far removed from contemporary English in these provocative poems. (New edition with an afterword by David Dabydeen.)

Mahadai Das, *A Leaf in His Ear: Selected Poems*, 1-900715-59-7, £8.99
May 2007 This selected poems, discussed with Mahadai Das before her death, brings together all the poems from *I Want to be a Poetess of my People*, *My Finer Steel will Grow*, *Bones* and previously uncollected poems.

Kwame Dawes, *Impossible Flying*, 1-84523-039-6, £7.99
October 2006 Dawes's most personal and universal collection in its focus on family and human suffering. The poems deal with family, focusing primarily on the triangular relationship between the poet, his father and younger brother, though there is also a deeply moving acknowledgement of the rocklike unconditionality of a mother's love and care for her family's wounded souls.

Delores Gauntlett, *The Watertank Revisited*, 1-84523-009-4, £7.99
A brother held at gunpoint, a mother paralyzed at her son's encounter with authority, and citizens in battle with the police and military are among the deeply disturbing and moving images rendered in this unflinching collection of poetry about contemporary Jamaica. The beautiful landscape and endurance of the Jamaican people are vividly described in this engaging collection from a rising Caribbean poet.

Nicolas Guillén, *Yoruba from Cuba: Selected Poems of Nicolas Guillén* translated by Salvador Ortiz-Carboneres 1-900715-97-X, £9.99
This dual language selection of Cuba's most outstanding poet, Nicolás Guillén, covers the wide range of his work, in a translation that captures the colloquial vigour and incantatory rhythms of Guillén's language.

Laurence Lieberman, *Carib's Leap*, 1-84523-022-1, £12.99
Carib's Leap brings together work from a dozen previous collections, and major new poems including those on the Big Drum Dance of Carriacou, poems that are alight with almost forty years of imaginative involvement with the Caribbean.

Marina Maxwell, *Decades to Ama*, 1-84523-017-5, £9.99
These poems, which date from the 1960s to the present, include lyrical paeans to the enduring, African-born creativity of the Caribbean people, dirges for the recurrent wreckage of hopes and warrior songs against the forces of neo-colonialism and phallocentrism. In them images of destruction and regeneration vie with equal power. At the heart of a quest for an authentic Caribbean politics and culture is a journey, 'thirty-how-much years of labour in this archipelago of stones' by a woman who is truly an elemental force in Caribbean writing.

Velma Pollard, *Leaving Traces*, 1-84523-021-3, £7.99
Ranging over the Jamaican and Caribbean past and the encroachments of a turbulent world, Velma Pollard's poems return always to the quiet touchstones of love and friendship. As the middle years hurry past, her poems explore what is important, what might survive.

Raymond Ramcharitar, *American Fall*, 1-84523-043-4, £7.99
February 2007 A thoroughly individual voice, with a capacity for writing verse narratives that reverberate like the best short stories, dramatic monologues that skilfully create other voices, and lyric poems that get inside the less obvious byways of emotion.

Heather Royes, *Days and Nights of the Blue Iguana*, 1-84523-019-1, £7.99
Though they traverse the wider Caribbean and beyond, Heather Royes' centre of gravity is always Jamaica ('No exile — small sabbaticals') which arouses in her both love and exasperation. Ancestors — a nomadic family 'wandering up

and down the islands', family and place are described with a painterly, compassionate eye for telling detail. The collection contains a generous selection from her first book of poems, *The Caribbean Raj*.

Dorothea Smartt, *Connecting Medium*, 1-900715-50-3, £7.99
Connecting Medium links the past to the present, the Caribbean to England, mothers to fathers. Here are poems about identity and culture, past generations and the future and a powerful sequence of poems about a black Medusa.

Rommi Smith, *Mornings and Midnights*, 1-900715-95-3, £7.99
February 2007 Rommi Smith creates the voice and world of legendary diva Gloria Silver in all her feisty sensuality. Through Gloria's journey of memory, much is said about the nature of performance and the sometimes ironic distance between the singer and the song.

Donna Weir-Soley, *First Rain*, 1-84523-033-7, £7.99
This is a spirit journey to pull together the necessary fragments, the record of a struggle towards wholeness. Aided by the words of her parable-speaking elders and ancestors, these poems build a vision of the Jamaican past as a guide to surviving the travails of an American present.

Gwyneth Barber Wood, *The Garden of Forgetting*, 1-84523-007-8, £7.99
These poems explore the life-shattering loss of a father and a husband. The relationship between inner feelings and the physical environment figures prominently as the poems, written in standard English and traditional verse forms, incorporate intensely Jamaican details and metaphors.

Recent & forthcoming fiction
by women writers

Opal Palmer Adisa, *Until Judgement Comes*, 1-84523-042-6, £8.99
November 2006 Sensitive and imaginative explorations of the mystery that is the male psyche. A collection that moves the heart and head, but above all is in love with telling stories — stories within stories, the reworkings of Jamaican folktales, tall tales and myths.

Jacqueline Bishop, *The River's Song*, 1-84523-038-8, £8.99
October 2006 Jacqueline Bishop invests the coming-of-age novel with a fresh, individual quality of voice, exploring her main character's sexual awakening and growing consciousness of Jamaica's class divisions, endemic violence and the new spectre of HIV-AIDS.

Jane Bryce, *Chameleon*, 1-84523-041-8, £7.99
December 2006 Stories that explore a Nigerian childhood and adolescence and the tensions between the pleasures of being an outsider and the desire to belong. Stories that make the crossing to the Caribbean with an awareness of how much of Africa was already there.

Myriam J. A. Chancy, *The Scorpion's Claw*, 1-900715-91-0, £8.99
Set in the chaotic aftermath of the fall of Baby Doc, resistance, recovery and re-creation go to the heart of this novel, which tells the past and present of two generations of Haitians.

Marcia Douglas, *Notes from a Writer's Book of Cures and Spells*, 1-84523-016-7, £8.99
Flamingo, a young Jamaican writer, finds her life becoming enmeshed with those of her characters, and when through poverty, emigration and Jamaica's political upheavals this fictional family is dispersed, one of the characters solicits Flamingo's help to bring them back together.

Beryl Gilroy, *The Green Grass Tango*, 1-900715-47-3, £7.99
Set in a London park amongst a diverse multi-racial community of dog-walkers and bench-sitters, this is comedy about identity, ageing, loneliness, love and dogs.

Denise Harris, *In Remembrance of Her*, 1-900715-99-6, £9.99
Set in Guyana, the novel begins with a murder whose motivation seems incomprehensible. What Harris's novel reveals is a wilfully forgetful society which needs to find compassion for the restless dead if the cycle of cruelty and suffering is to be broken.

Cherie Jones, *The Burning Bush Women*, 1-900715-58-9, £8.99
In these truthtelling, strange, funny and tragic stories, set in Barbados and the USA, Cherie Jones weaves paths through the joys and suffering of women's lives, dealing with love, magic and a deep connectedness between women.

Karen King-Aribisala, *The Hangman's Game*, 1-84523-046-9, £8.99
January 2007 A slave rebellion in nineteenth century Guyana and a military dictatorship in recent Nigeria intercut and merge in unsettling ways as the characters in the historical novel-within-a novel erupt into their Caribbean author's life in Nigeria.

Alecia McKenzie, *Stories from Yard*, 1-900715-62-7, £7.99
Fear and bitterness pollute the ground from which the young female characters of these stories must struggle to grow. With many 'bad seeds' of sexual violence, lies and prejudice taking root around them, their blossoming is always under threat.

Jennifer Rahim, *Songster and Other Stories*, 1-84523-048-5, £7.99
October 2006 Rahim's stories move between the present and the past to make sense of the tensions between image and reality in contemporary Trinidad.

Ryhaan Shah, *A Silent Life*, 1-84523-002-7, £8.99
Aleyah Hassan explores the mystery that surrounds her grandmother, Nani, in this tale of cross-generational revolutionary politics. Throughout this novel, family secrets are portrayed with both social realism and poetic imagination, and themes of class, race, and gender are explored incisively.

www.peepaltreepress.com